Traveling Leaves You Speechless.
Then Turns You Into a Storyteller.

- Ibn Battuta-

This book belongs to:

_____

DAILY AGENDA

Location: _____   Date: _____

Time:	Activity:

TOP 3 PLACES TO SEE OR THINGS TO DO:

_____

_____

_____

_____

Look at the stars lighting up the sky:
no one of them stays in the same place.

Seneca

DAILY AGENDA

Location: _____ Date: _____

Time:	Activity:

TOP 3 PLACES TO SEE OR THINGS TO DO:

_____

_____

_____

_____

Adventure is worthwhile.

Aristotle

DAILY AGENDA

Location: _____   Date: _____

Time:	Activity:

TOP 3 PLACES TO SEE OR THINGS TO DO:

_____

_____

_____

_____

Travelling leaves you speechless.
Then turns you into a Storyteller.

Ibn Battuta

DAILY AGENDA

Location: _____   Date: _____

Time:	Activity:

TOP 3 PLACES TO SEE OR THINGS TO DO:

_____

_____

_____

_____

Don't tell me how educated you are, tell me how much you travelled.

Mohammed

DAILY AGENDA

Location: _____   Date: _____

Time:	Activity:

TOP 3 PLACES TO SEE OR THINGS TO DO:

_____

_____

_____

_____

Travel, in the younger sort, is a part of education,
in the elder, a part of experience.

Francis Bacon

DAILY AGENDA

Location: _____ Date: _____

Time:	Activity:

TOP 3 PLACES TO SEE OR THINGS TO DO:

A good traveler has no fixed plans
and is not intent on arriving.

Lao Tzu

DAILY AGENDA

Location: _____ Date: _____

Time:	Activity:

TOP 3 PLACES TO SEE OR THINGS TO DO:

_____

_____

_____

_____

_____

Experience, travel, these are as education in themselves.

Euripides

DAILY AGENDA

Location: Date:

Time:	Activity:

TOP 3 PLACES TO SEE OR THINGS TO DO:

Travel brings power and love back into your life.

Rumi

DAILY AGENDA

Location: _____ Date: _____

Time:	Activity:

TOP 3 PLACES TO SEE OR THINGS TO DO:

_____

_____

_____

_____

The world is a book, and those who don't travel
read only one page.

St. Augustine

DAILY AGENDA

Location: _____   Date: _____

Time:	Activity:

TOP 3 PLACES TO SEE OR THINGS TO DO:

_____

_____

_____

_____

A journey of a thousand miles must begin
with a single step.

Lao Tzu

DAILY AGENDA

Location: _____   Date: _____

Time:	Activity:

TOP 3 PLACES TO SEE OR THINGS TO DO:

_____

_____

_____

_____

He who does not travel does not know the value of men.

Moorish proverb

DAILY AGENDA

Location: _____   Date: _____

Time:	Activity:

TOP 3 PLACES TO SEE OR THINGS TO DO:

_____

_____

_____

_____

_____

Voyage, travel and change of place impart vigor.

Seneca

DAILY AGENDA

Location: Date:

Time:	Activity:

TOP 3 PLACES TO SEE OR THINGS TO DO:

Empty-handed I entered the world, barefoot I leave it.
My coming, my going - two simple happenings, that got entangled.

Kozan Ichikyo

DAILY AGENDA

Location: _____ Date: _____

Time:	Activity:

TOP 3 PLACES TO SEE OR THINGS TO DO:

_____

_____

_____

_____

_____

He who returns from a journey is not the same as he who left.

Chinese proverb

DAILY AGENDA

Location: _____   Date: _____

Time:	Activity:

TOP 3 PLACES TO SEE OR THINGS TO DO:

_____

_____

_____

_____

It does not matter how slowly you go
as long as you do not stop.

Confucius

DAILY AGENDA

Location: _____   Date: _____

Time:	Activity:

TOP 3 PLACES TO SEE OR THINGS TO DO:

_____

_____

_____

_____

People travel to wonder at the height of the mountains, at the huge waves of the seas, at the long course of the rivers, at the vast compass of the ocean, at the circular motion of the stars, and yet they pass by themselves without wondering..

St. Augustine

DAILY AGENDA

Location: _____ Date: _____

Time:	Activity:

TOP 3 PLACES TO SEE OR THINGS TO DO:

_____

_____

_____

_____

Travel makes one modest.
You see what a tiny place you occupy in the world.

Gustav Flaubert

DAILY AGENDA

Location: _____   Date: _____

Time:	Activity:

TOP 3 PLACES TO SEE OR THINGS TO DO:

_____

_____

_____

_____

To travel is to live.

Hans Christian Andersen

DAILY AGENDA

Location: _____ Date: _____

Time:	Activity:

TOP 3 PLACES TO SEE OR THINGS TO DO:

_____

_____

_____

_____

Do not follow where the path may lead.
Go instead where there is no path and leave a trail.

Ralph Waldo Emseron

DAILY AGENDA

Location: _____   Date: _____

Time:	Activity:

TOP 3 PLACES TO SEE OR THINGS TO DO:

_____

_____

_____

Take only memories, leave only footprints.

Chief Seattle

DAILY AGENDA

Location: _____   Date: _____

Time:	Activity:

TOP 3 PLACES TO SEE OR THINGS TO DO:

_____

_____

_____

_____

Travel only with thy equals or thy betters,
if there are none, travel alone.

The Dhammapada

DAILY AGENDA

Location: _____   Date: _____

Time:	Activity:

TOP 3 PLACES TO SEE OR THINGS TO DO:

_____

_____

_____

_____

Our deeds still travel with us from afar,
and what we have been makes us what we are.

George Eliot

DAILY AGENDA

Location: Date:

Time:	Activity:

TOP 3 PLACES TO SEE OR THINGS TO DO:

When you're traveling, ask the traveler for advice -
not someone who'se lameness keeps him in one place.

Rumi

DAILY AGENDA

Location: _____   Date: _____

Time:	Activity:

TOP 3 PLACES TO SEE OR THINGS TO DO:

_____

_____

_____

_____

The autumn leaves are falling like rain. Although my neighbors are all barbarians. And you, you are a thousand miles away.
There are always two cups at my table.

Tang Dynasty Poem

DAILY AGENDA

Location: _____   Date: _____

Time:	Activity:

TOP 3 PLACES TO SEE OR THINGS TO DO:

_____

_____

_____

_____

A ship in harbor is safe, but that is not what ships are built for.

John A. Shedd

DAILY AGENDA

Location: _____   Date: _____

Time:	Activity:

TOP 3 PLACES TO SEE OR THINGS TO DO:

_____

_____

_____

_____

The use of traveling is to regulate imagination by reality,
and instead of thinking how things may be, to see them as they are.

Samuel Johnson

DAILY AGENDA

Location: Date:

Time:	Activity:

TOP 3 PLACES TO SEE OR THINGS TO DO:

The real voyage of discovery consist not in seeing new landscapes, but in having new eyes.

Marcel Proust

DAILY AGENDA

Location: _____ Date: _____

Time:	Activity:

TOP 3 PLACES TO SEE OR THINGS TO DO:

_____

_____

_____

_____

A man of ordinary talent will always be ordinary, whether he travels or not, but a man of superior talent will go to pieces if he remains forever in the same place.

Wolfgang Amadeus Mozart

DAILY AGENDA

Location: Date:

Time:	Activity:

TOP 3 PLACES TO SEE OR THINGS TO DO:

Roam abroad in the world, and take thy fill of its enjoyments
before the day shall come when thou must quit it for good.

Saadi

DAILY AGENDA

Location: Date:

Time:	Activity:

TOP 3 PLACES TO SEE OR THINGS TO DO:

The man who seeks to educate himself must first read
and then travel in order to correct what he has learned.

Casanova

DAILY AGENDA

Location: _____   Date: _____

Time:	Activity:

TOP 3 PLACES TO SEE OR THINGS TO DO:

_____

_____

_____

_____

Plunge boldly into the thick of life, and seize it where you will, it is always interesting.

Johann Wolfang von Goethe

DAILY AGENDA

Location: _____   Date: _____

Time:	Activity:

TOP 3 PLACES TO SEE OR THINGS TO DO:

The bold adventurer succeeds the best.

Ovid

DAILY AGENDA

Location: _____ Date: _____

Time:	Activity:

TOP 3 PLACES TO SEE OR THINGS TO DO:

The journey itself is my home.

Matsuo Bash

DAILY AGENDA

Location: _____ Date: _____

Time:	Activity:

TOP 3 PLACES TO SEE OR THINGS TO DO:

_____

_____

_____

_____

Walking 10-thousand miles of world is better than reading 10-thousand scrolls of books.

Chinese proverb

DAILY AGENDA

Location: _____ Date: _____

Time:	Activity:

TOP 3 PLACES TO SEE OR THINGS TO DO:

_____

_____

_____

_____

Traveling is almost like talking with men of other countries.

René Descartes

DAILY AGENDA

Location: _____   Date: _____

Time:	Activity:

TOP 3 PLACES TO SEE OR THINGS TO DO:

_____

_____

_____

_____

He who is outside his door has the hardest part of his journey behind him.

Dutch proverb

DAILY AGENDA

Location: _____   Date: _____

Time:	Activity:

TOP 3 PLACES TO SEE OR THINGS TO DO:

_____

_____

_____

_____

I was not born for one corner.
The whole world is my native land.

Seneca

DAILY AGENDA

Location: _____   Date: _____

Time:	Activity:

TOP 3 PLACES TO SEE OR THINGS TO DO:

_____

_____

_____

_____

Only he that has traveled the road knows where the holes are deep.

Chinese proverb

DAILY AGENDA

Location: _____ Date: _____

Time:	Activity:

TOP 3 PLACES TO SEE OR THINGS TO DO:

_____

_____

_____

_____

To shut your eyes is to travel.

Emily Dickinson

DAILY AGENDA

Location: _____ Date: _____

Time:	Activity:

TOP 3 PLACES TO SEE OR THINGS TO DO:

If you can't live loner, live deeper.

Italian proverb

DAILY AGENDA

Location: _____   Date: _____

Time:	Activity:

TOP 3 PLACES TO SEE OR THINGS TO DO:

_____

_____

_____

_____

It is better to travel than to arrive.

Buddha

DAILY AGENDA

Location: _____   Date: _____

Time:	Activity:

TOP 3 PLACES TO SEE OR THINGS TO DO:

_____

_____

_____

_____

Better to see something once than hear about it
a thousand times.

Uzbek proverb

DAILY AGENDA

Location: _____ Date: _____

Time:	Activity:

TOP 3 PLACES TO SEE OR THINGS TO DO:

_____

_____

_____

_____

No road is long with good company.

Turkish proverb

DAILY AGENDA

Location: _____ Date: _____

Time:	Activity:

TOP 3 PLACES TO SEE OR THINGS TO DO:

_____

_____

_____

_____

I tramp a perpetual journey.

Walt Whitman

DAILY AGENDA

Location: _____   Date: _____

Time:	Activity:

TOP 3 PLACES TO SEE OR THINGS TO DO:

_____

_____

_____

_____

How can you wonder your travels do you no good,
when you carry yourself around with you?

Socrates

DAILY AGENDA

Location: _____   Date: _____

Time:	Activity:

TOP 3 PLACES TO SEE OR THINGS TO DO:

_____

_____

_____

_____

I think one travels more usefully when they travel alone,
because they reflect more.

Thomas Jefferson

DAILY AGENDA

Location: _____   **Date:** _____

Time:	Activity:

TOP 3 PLACES TO SEE OR THINGS TO DO:

_____

_____

_____

_____

_____

If you really want to escape the things that harass you,
what you're needing is not to be in a different place
but to be a different person.

Seneca

DAILY AGENDA

Location: _____   Date: _____

Time:	Activity:

TOP 3 PLACES TO SEE OR THINGS TO DO:

_____

_____

_____

_____

The health of the eye seems to demand a horizon.
We are never tired, so long as we can see far enough.

Ralph Waldo Emerson

DAILY AGENDA

Location: _____   Date: _____

Time:	Activity:

TOP 3 PLACES TO SEE OR THINGS TO DO:

For walk where we will, we tread upon some story.

Marcus Tullius Cicero

Made in the USA
Middletown, DE
03 June 2025

76504151R00064